ROMANTIC LOVE STORY
PART 1

WHISPERS OF LOVE

ASTRA AUDEN

ACKNOWLEDGEMENTS

With heartfelt gratitude, I would like to thank my loving family, closest friends, and colleagues for their unwavering support, encouragement, and understanding. Your belief in my ability to bring these tales to life has been my greatest motivation.

Your insights have been crucial in shaping these narratives and ensuring they resonate with readers. Your dedication to excellence has been invaluable. I am immensely deeply grateful to you all for providing honest and constructive feedback. Your enthusiasm and engagement are the driving force behind my writing, and I am humbled by your support.

Thank you all.

©2024 Astra Auden. All rights reserved.

INTRODUCTION

Discover the magic of love in every chapter with the *"Whispers of Love"* series, a heartwarming collection of romantic stories designed to captivate and inspire. Each book in this enchanting series contains approximately 20 short love stories, each unique in its own way but united by the universal theme of love.

From the first blush of attraction to the enduring promise of forever, these tales explore the myriad ways love manifests in our lives. Whether you're a hopeless romantic, a skeptic seeking to be convinced, or simply someone who enjoys a good love story, there's something for everyone in this series.

Each story is crafted with care, designed to evoke emotions and leave a lasting impression. They are perfect for a quick read when you need a pick-me-up, a comforting companion on a rainy day, or a bedtime story to remind you of the beauty of love.

So, embark on a journey of love and discovery with the *"Whispers of Love"* series. Let these stories fill your heart with warmth, remind you of the power of love, and inspire you to believe in the magic of happily ever after.

CONTENTS

ACKNOWLEDGEMENTS 2
INTRODUCTION 3
CONTENTS 4

    Story 1：Sweet Melodies of Love 5
    Story 2：Embracing Warmth: A Tale of Cozy Affection 8
    Story 3：Beneath the Starlit Sky: A Tale of Endless Love 10
    Story 4：Silent Harmony: A Tale of Unspoken Understanding 12
    Story 5：Sparks of Love: A European Romance 15
    Story 6：You Are My Human Ideal 17
    Story 7：Years Like a Melody 19
    Story 8：The Gentle Embrace of Venice 21
    Story 9：The Depths of Passion: A Tale of Deep Affection in Paris 24
    Story 10：Lunar Love: A Tale of Moonlit Affection in Venice 27
    Story 11：Love Across Time: A Tale of Enchanting Cities 30
    Story 12：Destined by Three Lives: A Tale of Eternal Bond 33
    Story 13：Love Song of 1990: A Timeless Melody 35
    Story 14：Riverside of Longing: A Tale of European Romance 37
    Story 15：The Eternal Bond of Elena and Lucian 40
    Story 16：Charming Moments that Enchanted the City: The Tale of Elena and Lucian 43
    Story 17：Enchanted Ecstasy 46
    Story 18：Soul Mates Across the Alps 49
    Story 19：Eternal Love Affair 52
    Story 20：Sweet Surprise Attack 54

Story 1: Sweet Melodies of Love

In the quaint village of Lille, nestled in the heart of France, a young woman named Claire Delacroix had always believed in the magic of love. With her golden curls cascading over her shoulders and eyes that sparkled like emeralds, Claire worked as a pianist at the charming Café Rouge, a local hotspot known for its live music and exquisite pastries. The café was a sanctuary where the scent of freshly baked croissants mingled with the melodies of the grand piano, creating an ambiance that was both cozy and enchanting.

One crisp autumn evening, as the leaves painted the town in hues of red and gold, the café was bustling with patrons eager to escape the chill outside. Claire sat at the piano, her fingers dancing over the keys, weaving a symphony that seemed to warm the souls of all who listened. It was during one of these performances that she first noticed him—a tall, dashing man with a beard that framed his face like a masterpiece and eyes that held the depth of a thousand unspoken stories.
His name was Lucian de Saint-Claude, a renowned cellist from Paris who had come to Lille for a brief musical collaboration. As Lucian stood near the entrance, captivated by Claire's playing, a soft smile tugged at the corners of his lips. He had never heard anything so beautiful, so pure, that it seemed to touch the very essence of his being.

The following night, Lucian returned to Café Rouge, this time with the intention of meeting the enchanting pianist. As fate would have it, Claire took a brief intermission between sets and found herself face to face with the man who had stolen her thoughts the previous evening.
"Your music is like nothing I've ever heard," Lucian said, his voice as smooth as velvet. "It's as if every note carries a story."
Claire blushed, feeling a warmth spread through her chest. "Thank you," she replied, her voice barely above a whisper. "It's always a joy to share my music with others."

From that moment on, Lucian and Claire's bond grew stronger with each passing day. They spoke of their love for music, their dreams, and their aspirations. They discovered they had an uncanny ability to finish each other's sentences and a mutual admiration for the simpler pleasures in life, like walking through the fields of lavender during sunset or sharing a croissant and coffee at Café Rouge.

One particular evening, as the café prepared to close, Lucian asked Claire to accompany him to the local violin shop. Intrigued, she followed him, wondering what he had planned. Inside the quaint shop, adorned with instruments that seemed to whisper tales of their own, Lucian picked up a cello and began to play. His music was deep, rich, and emotional, complementing Claire's piano playing in a way that felt destined.

When he finished, he turned to her, his eyes filled with sincerity. "Claire, every moment I've spent with you has been like a melody, harmonious and perfect. I want to share every note of my life with you."

Tears of joy welled up in Claire's eyes as she realized the significance of his words. "Lucian, I feel the same way. Every beat of my heart resonates with yours."

He took her hand, leading her to the center of the shop, and placed a delicate silver ring on her finger, inscribed with the words "Eternal Melody." It was a symbol of their bond, a promise of forever intertwined lives.

Their love continued to blossom, filling their days with laughter, music, and an unspoken understanding that transcended words. They married in a small, intimate ceremony at Café Rouge, surrounded by friends, family, and the melodies that had brought them together.

Years later, as they sat together on a bench overlooking the picturesque countryside, hand in hand, Claire and Lucian smiled, their hearts full of gratitude. They had lived a life filled with sweet melodies of love, each note playing a part in the beautiful symphony of their everlasting journey.

And so, in the quaint village of Lille, their love story became a legend, reminding everyone who passed through of the magic that happens when two souls find each other, and together, create the sweetest melodies of all.

Story 2: Embracing Warmth: A Tale of Cozy Affection

In the picturesque village of Salzburg, Austria, nestled amidst the breathtaking Alps and the historic charm of its cobblestone streets, lived a young woman named Elara von Steinberg. With her cascading waves of chestnut hair and eyes that mirrored the deep blue of the Salzach River, Elara worked as a seamstress at the local boutique, weaving intricate designs that seemed to capture the essence of love and warmth.

One crisp winter evening, as snowflakes danced in the twilight, Elara closed up her shop and made her way home. She wrapped her woolen scarf tighter around her neck, trying to fend off the biting chill that seemed to seep into her bones. It was on this frosty night that she first noticed him—a tall, broad-shouldered man with a kind smile and eyes that sparkled with warmth, standing outside her apartment building.

His name was Franz Lechner, a recent arrival in Salzburg, having moved from Munich to take a position as a professor of classical literature at the local university. Franz had been drawn to Elara's boutique by the beautiful garments displayed in the window and had inadvertently found himself waiting for her to emerge, captivated by her gentle demeanor and the way she seemed to radiate warmth even in the coldest of winters.

As Elara approached, Franz introduced himself, his voice as smooth as hot chocolate on a winter's day. "I couldn't help but notice your shop," he said, gesturing towards the boutique. "Your designs are incredible. They seem to tell stories of warmth and love."

Elara blushed, feeling a warmth spread through her cheeks that had nothing to do with the cold. "Thank you," she replied, her voice tinged with shyness. "It's always a joy to create something beautiful."

From that moment on, Franz and Elara's bond grew stronger with each passing day. They met for walks through the snow-covered parks, shared steaming cups of glühwein at the local Christmas market, and spent countless hours discussing literature, art, and the simple pleasures of life.

Franz was captivated by Elara's kindness and creativity, while Elara found solace in Franz's wisdom and gentle nature.

One particular evening, as the village was bathed in the soft glow of twinkling fairy lights, Franz took Elara to a cozy, intimate restaurant overlooking the Salzach River. The ambiance was warm and inviting, with the scent of roasted chestnuts and mulled wine filling the air. As they sat together, their hands brushing against each other's, Franz reached into his coat pocket and pulled out a small, beautifully wrapped box.

"Elara," he began, his voice filled with emotion, "from the moment I met you, I felt an inexplicable connection. You bring warmth to my life, even in the coldest of winters. I want to spend every moment with you, sharing in the joy and sorrow, the laughter and the tears. Will you let me?"

Elara's eyes filled with tears of joy as she realized the significance of Franz's words. "Franz," she replied, her voice trembling with emotion, "you have brought light into my life. I want to embark on this journey with you, to face the world together, hand in hand."

Franz opened the box, revealing a delicate silver locket etched with intricate designs of vines and flowers. Inside, a tiny photo of the two of them, captured during one of their snowy walks, smiled back at them. It was a symbol of their bond, a promise of forever intertwined lives.

As the night wore on, Franz and Elara made their way back to her apartment, their hearts full of love and anticipation. They sat together on the couch, wrapped in a soft, cozy blanket, their bodies pressed close, each feeling the warmth of the other's embrace. It was in these moments of quiet intimacy, of sharing in the simple pleasures of life, that they found true happiness.

And so, in the picturesque village of Salzburg, Franz and Elara's love story became a tale of cozy affection, a reminder that true love is not just about grand gestures and romantic escapades, but about the simple, profound joy of being together, of finding warmth in each other's embrace.

Story 3: Beneath the Starlit Sky: A Tale of Endless Love

In the quaint village of Grasse, nestled in the heart of the French Riviera, where the scent of lavender fills the air and the Mediterranean Sea whispers secrets to the shore, lived a young woman named Claire Dumas. With her cascading waves of chestnut hair and eyes that mirrored the deep blue of the night sky, Claire was known for her love of astronomy, spending countless hours gazing at the stars with a telescope her grandfather had given her.

One fateful evening, as Claire stood on the hill overlooking the village, her gaze fixed on the constellation of Orion, she noticed a man standing at the edge of the hill, his eyes also turned to the heavens. He was tall and broad-shouldered, with hair as dark as a raven's wing and eyes that sparkled like the stars themselves. His name was Lucas Chevalier, a visiting astronomer from Paris, here to attend a conference on celestial phenomena.
Lucas had been drawn to Grasse not only for its beauty but also for the clarity of its night skies, perfect for stargazing. As he observed the stars, he couldn't help but notice Claire, her face illuminated by the glow of the telescope's lens, her eyes alight with wonder. He approached her, his heart pounding with anticipation.

"Excuse me," Lucas began, his voice a gentle whisper in the cool night air. "I couldn't help but notice your telescope. Are you an astronomer?"
Claire turned to face him, her eyes widening in surprise. "Not professionally," she replied, her voice tinged with shyness. "But I do love stargazing. It's like being able to touch the universe."
Lucas smiled, feeling an inexplicable connection to this woman who shared his passion for the stars. "I'm Lucas Chevalier," he introduced himself. "I'm here for a conference on celestial phenomena. May I join you?"

Claire nodded, feeling a warmth spread through her that had nothing to do with the night's gentle breeze. From that moment on, Lucas and Claire spent every clear night together, their eyes fixed on the stars, their hearts intertwined in a bond of shared wonder.

As their relationship deepened, so did their love for the stars. Lucas introduced Claire to the wonders of the cosmos, pointing out constellations and planets she had never seen before. In return, Claire shared her own insights, her love for the stars as a source of inspiration and comfort.

One particular evening, as they lay together on a blanket beneath the starlit sky, Lucas reached into his pocket and pulled out a small, intricately designed box. "Claire," he began, his voice filled with emotion, "from the moment I met you, I felt an inexplicable connection. You have brought light into my life, like the stars themselves. I want to spend every moment with you, exploring the universe together."

Claire's eyes filled with tears of joy as she realized the significance of Lucas's words. "Lucas," she replied, her voice trembling with emotion, "you have shown me the wonders of the cosmos in a way I never imagined. I want to embark on this journey with you, to face the world together, hand in hand."

Lucas opened the box, revealing a delicate silver necklace with a pendant shaped like a star, its surface etched with the constellations of their favorite stars. "This is for you," he said, his voice soft but filled with conviction. "A symbol of our bond, a promise of forever intertwined lives."

Claire's heart swelled with love as she put on the necklace, feeling the warmth of Lucas's love and the magic of the stars. They lay together, their bodies pressed close, their hearts beating in unison, beneath the starlit sky, a tapestry of endless love.

And so, in the quaint village of Grasse, beneath the starlit sky, Lucas and Claire's love story became a tale of endless love, a reminder that true love is not just about grand gestures and romantic escapades, but about the simple, profound joy of being together, of sharing in the wonder of the universe.

Story 4: Silent Harmony: A Tale of Unspoken Understanding

In the picturesque city of Salzburg, Austria, renowned for its Baroque architecture and musical heritage, lived a young woman named Sophia Weber. Sophia was a talented pianist, her fingers dancing over the keys with a grace and precision that captivated audiences. She was known for her ability to convey deep emotion through her music, a gift she had honed since childhood.

Across the city, in a quaint little café named "Der Harmonie," worked a young man named Markus Mozart. Markus was not related to the famous composer, but he had inherited a love for music from his ancestors, who were avid musicians and collectors of classical pieces. He was a skilled violinist, with a talent for improvisation that never failed to amaze his listeners.

Sophia and Markus had never met, despite living in the same city and sharing a passion for music. Their worlds were as separate as the notes on a grand staff, until one fateful evening at a charity concert organized by the Salzburg Philharmonic Orchestra.

The concert hall was filled with the rich, melodic sounds of various instruments, each note weaving a tapestry of harmony. Sophia was to perform a solo piece, her fingers poised over the keys, ready to bring the audience to tears with her rendering of Beethoven's "Moonlight Sonata." Markus, who had been invited to perform as part of a string quartet, sat in the wings, his violin case at his side, waiting for his turn.

As Sophia began to play, the melody flowed through the concert hall like a gentle stream, each note carrying an unspoken emotion. Markus, captivated by the music, closed his eyes and let the notes wash over him. He felt an inexplicable connection to the pianist, a sense of unspoken understanding that transcended words.

When Sophia's performance ended, the audience erupted into applause. Markus, still caught in the spell of the music, found himself standing, his hands clapping instinctively. As the applause faded, he turned to see Sophia standing at the piano, her eyes meeting his for the first time. In that brief, fleeting moment, a silent harmony was born, a bond of unspoken understanding that neither could explain.

The following day, Markus found himself unable to shake the memory of Sophia's performance. He decided to visit the café where she was known to frequent, hoping to catch a glimpse of her. As he walked through the door, he saw her sitting at a corner table, her fingers tapping rhythmically on the tabletop.

Markus approached her, his heart pounding with anticipation. "Excuse me," he began, his voice barely above a whisper. "I couldn't help but notice your talent last night. You played beautifully."

Sophia looked up, her eyes widening in surprise. "Thank you," she replied, her voice tinged with shyness. "I couldn't help but notice your playing too. Your improvisations were incredible."

From that moment on, Sophia and Markus's worlds collided in a symphony of unspoken understanding. They spent countless hours together, discussing music, sharing their favorite pieces, and even collaborating on duets. Their bond grew stronger with each passing day, a silent harmony that needed no words to express its depth.

One evening, as they sat together in "Der Harmonie," Markus reached into his pocket and pulled out a small, intricately designed music box. "Sophia," he began, his voice filled with emotion, "since the day we met, you have brought music and joy into my life. This music box is a symbol of our bond, a reminder of the silent harmony we share."

Sophia's eyes filled with tears as she opened the music box, revealing a tiny ballet dancer that twirled to the tune of a classical melody. "Markus," she replied, her voice trembling with emotion, "you have shown me a world of music and unspoken understanding that I never knew existed. I want to embark on this journey with you, to create a symphony of love together."

And so, in the picturesque city of Salzburg, Sophia and Markus's love story became a tale of silent harmony, a reminder that true love is not just about grand gestures and romantic escapades, but about the simple, profound joy of being together, of sharing in the unspoken understanding that binds two souls forever.

Story 5: Sparks of Love: A European Romance

In the charming city of Paris, France, where the Seine River gently curves through the heart of the city and the Eiffel Tower stands as a testament to human ingenuity, lived a young woman named Claire Boulanger. Claire was a talented artist, known for her ability to capture the essence of life in her paintings. Her works were filled with vibrant colors and a sense of joy that seemed to leap off the canvas.

Across the city, in a quaint little bookstore called "Les Éclats d'Amour" (The Sparks of Love), worked a young man named Luc Delacroix. Luc was an avid reader and a poet, with a knack for crafting words that painted vivid pictures in the minds of his readers. His poems were filled with emotion and a deep understanding of the human condition.

Claire and Luc had never met, despite living in the same city and sharing a love for creativity. Their worlds were as separate as the pages of a book, until one rainy afternoon when fate 干预 ed.
Claire had been painting in Montmartre, her favorite place to find inspiration, when a sudden downpour forced her to seek shelter. She ran into "Les Éclats d'Amour," shaking the rain from her clothes and clutching her sketchbook close to her chest. Luc, who was busy arranging new titles on the shelves, looked up and saw her standing there, dripping wet but still radiating an air of grace.
"Bonjour," he greeted her warmly, offering her a towel to dry herself. "Welcome to Les Éclats d'Amour. Is there anything I can help you find?"
Claire smiled, her eyes lighting up as she took in the cozy atmosphere of the bookstore. "I was just looking for a place to shelter from the rain," she replied. "But I must say, your bookstore has a lovely name."

Luc chuckled. "Thank you. It's named after a poem I wrote. It's about the sparks of love that ignite between two souls, even in the most unlikely places."

Claire's eyes widened in surprise. "That's beautiful," she said softly. "I'm an artist, and I've always believed that creativity can spark connections between people."

Luc's interest was piqued. "Would you like to see my poems?" he asked, leading her to a corner of the bookstore where his works were displayed.

As Claire read Luc's poems, she felt a spark of recognition, a sense of connection that went beyond words. She could see the world through his eyes, feel the emotions he was trying to convey. And as Luc listened to Claire talk about her paintings, he was captivated by her passion and her ability to capture the beauty of life.

From that day on, Claire and Luc's worlds collided in a symphony of creativity and love. They spent countless hours together, discussing their art, sharing their inspirations, and even collaborating on a project that combined Luc's poetry with Claire's paintings.

One evening, as they sat together in a cozy café, Luc reached into his pocket and pulled out a small, beautifully crafted book. "Claire," he began, his voice filled with emotion, "since the day we met, you have brought creativity and joy into my life. This book is a collection of my poems, dedicated to you. It's a testament to the sparks of love that ignite between us."

Claire's eyes filled with tears as she took the book from his hands, flipping through the pages and reading the words that had once only existed in Luc's mind. "Luc," she replied, her voice trembling with emotion, "you have shown me a world of words and emotions that I never knew existed. I want to embark on this journey with you, to create a symphony of love and creativity together."

And so, in the charming city of Paris, Claire and Luc's love story became a tale of sparks of love, a reminder that true love is not just about grand gestures and romantic escapades, but about the simple, profound joy of being together, of sharing in the creative spark that ignites between two souls.

Story 6: You Are My Human Ideal

In the quaint village of Provence, nestled between rolling vineyards and sun-drenched lavender fields, lived a young woman named Claire Dubois. Claire was known for her kindness, her infectious laughter, and her unwavering optimism. She had a way of seeing the world through rose-colored glasses, finding beauty in even the most mundane of things. To the villagers, Claire was a beacon of light, a symbol of hope and joy.

Across the village, in a charming stone cottage with ivy-clad walls, lived a young man named Luc Delacroix. Luc was a talented musician, with a voice that could soothe the savagest of beasts and melt the hardest of hearts. He had a penchant for writing songs that captured the essence of human emotion, from the deepest joys to the darkest sorrows. Luc's music was his passion, his soul's expression, and his ticket to fame and fortune in the bustling city of Paris.

Though Claire and Luc lived in the same village, their worlds had never truly collided until one fateful summer evening at the village's annual harvest festival. As the sun dipped below the horizon, casting a golden glow upon the vineyards, the air was filled with the sweet melodies of Luc's guitar and the laughter of the villagers. Claire, drawn by the sound of Luc's music, found herself standing at the edge of the crowd, her heart pounding in her chest.

Luc noticed Claire immediately, her radiant smile standing out amidst the sea of faces. He felt an inexplicable pull towards her, as if she were the missing piece to his puzzle, the one person who could complete him. As he played his final chord, Luc's eyes met Claire's, and in that fleeting moment, a bond was forged, a connection that neither could fully understand but both knew was real.

From that evening on, Claire and Luc's lives became intertwined. They began to meet secretly, often under the cover of night, in the vineyards or by the river, where they could share their thoughts, dreams, and fears without fear of judgment. They discovered a shared passion for literature, art, and the simple joys of life, and their bond grew stronger with each passing day.

One evening, as they sat by the river, watching the stars twinkle above, Luc took a deep breath and turned to Claire. "Claire," he began, his voice filled with emotion, "from the moment I saw you, I knew that you were something special. You are my human ideal, the one person who makes me feel complete. I want to spend every moment of my life with you, exploring the world, creating music, and sharing our love with the universe."

Claire's eyes filled with tears as she listened to Luc's heartfelt words. She had never felt so understood, so loved, so truly seen. "Luc," she replied softly, her voice trembling with emotion, "you are my human ideal too. I have never felt so connected to someone, so in sync with their soul. I want to spend the rest of my life with you, creating memories, writing songs, and making music together."

And so, in the quaint village of Provence, surrounded by the beauty of nature and the love of their friends and family, Claire Dubois and Luc Delacroix exchanged vows of eternal love, promising to cherish each other for as long as they lived. They knew that their bond was special, a rare and precious gift that they would cherish and nurture for all eternity. Together, they would write their own love story, a story of two souls who found each other, who recognized each other as their human ideal, and who would spend the rest of their lives exploring the wonders of the world and the depths of their love.

Story 7: Years Like a Melody

In the picturesque town of Salzburg, Austria, where the rolling hills are adorned with vineyards and the air is filled with the sweet melodies of opera, lived a young woman named Elena Fischer. Elena was a talented pianist, with fingers that danced across the keys like a ballet dancer, weaving tales of love, sorrow, and joy through her music. She had a heart full of dreams and a soul that yearned for adventure, but most of all, she longed for a love that would transcend time and space, a love that would sing like a melody through the years.

In the same town, in a quaint cobblestone cottage near the Salzburg Cathedral, lived a young man named Karl Heim. Karl was an aspiring composer, with a mind full of ideas and a heart that burned with passion for his craft. He spent his days and nights writing symphonies, sonatas, and chamber music, each piece a reflection of his innermost thoughts and feelings. Karl had a deep-seated belief that music was the universal language, the one that could bridge the gap between people, heal wounds, and bring joy to even the darkest of days.

Though Elena and Karl lived in the same town, their paths had never truly crossed until one fateful evening at the Salzburg Festival. As the sun dipped below the horizon, casting a golden glow upon the city, the air was filled with the sweet melodies of an orchestra tuning up for the evening's performance. Elena, drawn by the sound of music, found herself standing in the crowd, her heart pounding in her chest. Karl, who was performing in the orchestra, noticed Elena immediately, her radiant smile standing out amidst the sea of faces.

From that evening on, Elena and Karl's lives became intertwined. They began to meet secretly, often under the cover of night, in the gardens of the Salzburg Cathedral or by the Salzach River, where they could share their thoughts, dreams, and fears without fear of judgment. They discovered a shared passion for music, art, and the simple joys of life, and their bond grew stronger with each passing day.

As the years went by, Elena and Karl's love blossomed, maturing like a fine wine, richer and deeper with each passing season. They married in a beautiful ceremony at the Salzburg Cathedral, surrounded by the sweet melodies of an orchestra playing Karl's composition, a symphony that captured the essence of their love.

Together, Elena and Karl traveled the world, performing their music and sharing their love with audiences around the globe. They lived in Paris, where they performed at the Louvre, in Vienna, where they danced in the gardens of Schönbrunn Palace, and in New York City, where they played their hearts out at Carnegie Hall. But no matter where they were, no matter how far they traveled, they always found their way back to Salzburg, the place where their love had first blossomed.

Years like a melody, Elena and Karl's love continued to grow, richer and deeper with each passing day.
They had children, grandchildren, and great-grandchildren, each generation adding their own unique melody to the symphony of their family. As they aged, they sat together in the gardens of their quaint cobblestone cottage, watching the sun dip below the horizon, their hands intertwined, their hearts full of gratitude for the love that had brought them together and sustained them through the years.

And so, in the picturesque town of Salzburg, where the rolling hills are adorned with vineyards and the air is filled with the sweet melodies of opera, Elena Fischer and Karl Heim lived out their love story, a story of two souls who found each other, who created a symphony of love that would sing through the years like a melody, a timeless and eternal testament to their enduring love.

Story 8: The Gentle Embrace of Venice

In the romantic city of Venice, where the waters whisper secrets and the sun sets in hues of pink and gold, lived a young woman named Elara. She had inherited her grandmother's charming canal-side café, "La Dolce Vita," a place where the aroma of freshly baked pastries and the sound of gentle laughter filled the air. Elara's heart was as delicate as the lace curtains that adorned the windows, and her smile was as warm as the sun on a spring morning.

One crisp autumn afternoon, a tall, distinguished man named Lucian arrived at La Dolce Vita. With his dark hair swept back in a casual yet elegant manner and eyes that sparkled like the Adriatic Sea, he seemed to belong to another era. Lucian was an artist, a painter searching for inspiration in the most enchanting cities of Europe. Venice, with its labyrinthine canals and historical architecture, had called to him like a siren's song.

Elara noticed Lucian immediately. His presence was calming, a gentle breeze in the midst of her bustling café. She approached him with a tray of her grandmother's famous tiramisu and a smile that lit up her entire being. "Buongiorno, signorino. Welcome to La Dolce Vita. May I interest you in a taste of our speciality?"
Lucian's gaze met hers, and for a moment, it felt as if the world around them ceased to exist. "Buongiorno, signorina. Your smile is more inviting than any menu. I would be delighted to try your tiramisu."

As days turned into weeks, Lucian became a regular at La Dolce Vita. He painted scenes of Venice's beauty from the café's window, capturing the essence of the city with every stroke of his brush. Elara, meanwhile, ran the café with a blend of efficiency and grace, always finding time to chat with Lucian or bring him a cup of hot chocolate just the way he liked it.
One evening, as the sun dipped below the horizon, painting the sky in hues of purple and orange, Lucian decided it was time to share his heart. He gently set aside his paintbrush and walked over to where Elara was

arranging flowers. "Elara, there is something I must tell you. From the first moment I saw you, you have brought a sense of peace and joy into my life. Your gentleness is like a soft melody that plays in my heart. Would you allow me to show you my world, not just through my paintings, but through my actions and words?"

Elara's cheeks flushed with a mix of surprise and delight. She had felt the same connection, a warmth that seemed to wrap around her like a cozy blanket. "Lucian, your words are as beautiful as your paintings. I would love to see your world, to share in your dreams and your inspirations."
Their relationship blossomed like the flowers that adorned La Dolce Vita. They wandered through Venice's narrow streets, hand in hand, exploring hidden courtyards and ancient bridges. Lucian painted Elara, capturing her essence in stroke after stroke, while Elara baked treats inspired by their adventures, sharing her love through food.

One moonlit night, they took a gondola ride through the canals. The water gleamed like silver, reflecting the stars above. Lucian reached into his pocket and pulled out a small, intricately carved box. "Elara, you have made my life richer, fuller. I want to spend every moment with you, exploring not just Venice, but the world and our hearts together. Will you marry me?"
Tears of joy sparkled in Elara's eyes as she nodded. "Yes, Lucian. I would be honored to share my life with you, to walk through this beautiful world with your hand in mine."
Their wedding was a celebration of love and gentleness, held in the café that had brought them together. Friends and family gathered, their hearts warm with the joy of seeing two souls unite. As they exchanged vows under a canopy of flowers and fairy lights, the city of Venice seemed to hum with approval, its waters whispering blessings.

And so, in the gentle embrace of Venice, Elara and Lucian began their life together, a life filled with love, art, and the simple, profound beauty of sharing every moment.

Story 9: The Depths of Passion: A Tale of Deep Affection in Paris

In the heart of Paris, a city renowned for its romance and history, lived a young woman named Claire. With her auburn hair cascading in soft waves and eyes that shimmered like the Seine at dusk, Claire was a painter, capturing the essence of life on canvas. She lived in a quaint apartment overlooking the river, where the gentle sound of water flowing under the bridges provided a soothing backdrop to her creative endeavors.

One fateful evening, Claire attended a gallery opening in the Montmartre district. The air was thick with the scent of fresh paint and the excitement of artists showcasing their work. It was there that she met Alexandre, a talented musician whose melodies could stir the soul and whose eyes held the depth of a thousand unspoken stories.

Alexandre was playing a haunting piano piece that seemed to pull Claire into another realm. The notes cascaded like a waterfall, each one striking her heart with a resounding echo. When the final chord resonated through the room, Claire found herself standing before him, unable to tear herself away. "Your music... it's like a journey through the soul," Claire whispered, her voice barely above a murmur.
Alexandre looked up, his eyes meeting hers with a warmth that melted her heart. "And your paintings... they tell stories that words cannot. It's as if we were meant to find each other."
From that moment, Claire and Alexandre's lives intertwined like the threads of a tapestry. They spent hours in Claire's apartment, her painting while he played, their creativity feeding each other's inspiration. The city of Paris became their backdrop, each corner and alleyway a testament to their deepening affection.

One rainy afternoon, as they sat by the window watching the rain dance upon the Seine, Alexandre took Claire's hands in his. "Claire, there is something I must share with you. Since we met, you have brought a light to my life that I never knew existed. Your passion for your art, your kindness, and your deep, abiding love for life have changed me. I want to spend every moment with you, exploring not just Paris, but the depths of our hearts together."

Claire's eyes filled with tears, her heart swelling with emotion. "Alexandre, I feel the same. You have become my muse, my guiding star. I cannot imagine a life without your music, your laughter, and your love."

As the days turned into weeks, and the weeks into months, their bond grew stronger. They traveled through the city, from the charming streets of Le Marais to the serene gardens of the Luxembourg Palace, each place a memory etched into their hearts. Alexandre composed pieces inspired by Claire's paintings, while Claire painted scenes inspired by his melodies, their art becoming a tapestry of their love.

One evening, as the sun dipped below the horizon, casting a golden glow over the Seine, Alexandre led Claire to a small, intimate restaurant on the riverbank. The air was thick with anticipation, the candles flickering softly as if in anticipation of what was to come.

"Claire," Alexandre began, his voice steady but filled with emotion, "I have come to realize that my love for you runs deeper than words can express. You are my soulmate, my everything. Will you marry me, and spend the rest of our lives exploring the depths of our passion and affection?"

Claire's heart swelled with joy, her eyes sparkling with tears of happiness. "Yes, Alexandre. I will marry you, and together we will navigate the journey of life, hand in hand, heart to heart."

Their wedding was a celebration of love and art, held in a quaint chapel near the Seine. Friends and family gathered, their hearts warm with the joy of seeing two souls unite. As they exchanged vows under a canopy of flowers and fairy lights, Paris seemed to hum with approval, its streets echoing their love.

And so, in the depths of Paris, Claire and Alexandre began their life together, a life filled with passion, creativity, and the profound beauty of sharing every moment with the one they loved most.

Story 10: Lunar Love: A Tale of Moonlit Affection in Venice

In the serene city of Venice, where the canals weave like silver threads through the heart of the city, lived a young woman named Elara. With her hair cascading in waves of chestnut and eyes that mirrored the deep blue of the Adriatic, Elara was a dreamer, her heart forever caught in the gentle embrace of the moon's soft light. She lived in a charming palazzo overlooking the Grand Canal, its ornate architecture a reflection of her own artistic soul.

One evening, as the sun dipped below the horizon and the first whispers of moonlight kissed the waters, Elara ventured out onto the canals. The city glowed with an ethereal beauty, the moonlight casting a silvery hue over the ancient buildings and cobblestone streets. It was on this enchanting night that she met Luca, a talented violinist whose melodies could weave through the soul like moonlight through the clouds.

Luca was performing a haunting piece on the Rialto Bridge, his violin singing out over the waters like a siren's call. Elara found herself drawn to the sound, her heart resonating with each note. She stood in the shadows, watching as the moonlight danced upon his shoulders, casting a halo of light around him. When the final note lingered in the air, Elara approached him, her heart pounding with a mix of awe and trepidation. "Your music... it's like moonlight, soft and ethereal, yet filled with an untold story," she said, her voice barely above a whisper.

Luca turned to her, his eyes reflecting the moonlight as they met hers. "And you, miss, you seem to carry the essence of the moon within you. It's as if we were meant to find each other under the lunar glow."
From that moment, Elara and Luca's lives became intertwined with the phases of the moon. They spent nights wandering through the labyrinthine streets of Venice, their footsteps echoing softly against the ancient cobblestones. Luca would play his violin, each note a tender brushstroke

upon Elara's heart, while she would share her dreams and aspirations, her voice a melody that sang in harmony with his.

One moonlit evening, as they sat by the waters of the Grand Canal, Luca took Elara's hands in his. "Elara, there is something I must share with you. Since we met, you have brought a light to my life that I never knew existed. Your passion for life, your kindness, and your deep, abiding love for the beauty of the world have changed me. I want to spend every moment with you, exploring not just Venice, but the depths of our hearts together."

Elara's heart swelled with emotion, her eyes sparkling with tears of happiness. "Luca, I feel the same. You have become my guiding star, my everything. I cannot imagine a life without your music, your laughter, and your love."

As the days turned into weeks, and the weeks into months, their bond grew stronger. They wandered through the city, from the serene squares of St. Mark's to the hidden gardens of Murano, each place a memory etched into their hearts by the soft glow of moonlight. Luca composed pieces inspired by Elara's dreams, while Elara painted scenes inspired by his melodies, their art becoming a tapestry of their love.

One evening, as the full moon cast its silvery glow over the city, Luca led Elara to a secluded spot on the canals, where a small gondola awaited. The air was thick with anticipation, the moonlight dancing upon the waters like a million diamonds.

"Elara," Luca began, his voice steady but filled with emotion, "I have come to realize that my love for you runs deeper than the waters of Venice, stronger than the tides. You are my soulmate, my everything. Will you marry me, and spend the rest of our lives exploring the depths of our affection under the soft glow of moonlight?"

Elara's heart swelled with joy, her eyes sparkling with tears of pure happiness. "Yes, Luca. I will marry you, and together we will navigate the journey of life, hand in hand, heart to heart, forever bathed in the gentle embrace of moonlight."

Their wedding was a celebration of love and art, held in a charming palazzo overlooking the Grand Canal. Friends and family gathered, their hearts warm with the joy of seeing two souls unite. As they exchanged vows under a canopy of flowers and fairy lights, Venice seemed to hum with approval, its canals echoing their love.

And so, in the serene city of Venice, Elara and Luca began their life together, a life filled with passion, creativity, and the profound beauty of sharing every moment with the one they loved most, forever bathed in the soft, ethereal glow of moonlight.

Story 11: Love Across Time: A Tale of Enchanting Cities

In the heart of Paris, a city known for its romance and timeless beauty, lived a young woman named Evelina De Clermont. Evelina, with her cascading waves of chestnut hair and eyes that mirrored the Seine on a sunny day, was a painter whose brushstrokes captured not just the essence of her surroundings but also the deep emotions harbored within her soul.

One fateful autumn evening, as the golden leaves danced down the Champs-Élysées, Evelina stumbled upon an old, abandoned bookstore tucked away in a narrow alley. The sign above, barely legible due to time's relentless embrace, read "Le Livre de Temps Perdu" – The Book of Lost Time. Intrigued, she pushed open the creaky door and stepped inside.

The air was thick with the scent of aged paper and forgotten stories. Dust particles floated lazily in the dim light filtering through grimy windows. Shelves, overloaded with tomes and manuscripts, seemed to stretch towards the ceiling in a labyrinthine embrace. Evelina wandered through the maze, her fingers brushing against spines that whispered secrets of centuries past.

In one corner, she found a leather-bound journal, its cover adorned with intricate carvings of intertwined hearts and roses. Opening it, she discovered it belonged to a man named Arnaud Duval, a poet from the early 1900s. Arnaud's words, passionate and profound, spoke of an undying love for a woman named Isabelle, whose image he described with such vividness that Evelina felt she could see her standing before her – a vision of ethereal beauty with eyes like the night sky and hair like spun gold.

Days turned into weeks as Evelina found herself returning to the bookstore, reading Arnaud's journal meticulously. She felt an inexplicable connection to the poet, as if his words were a bridge spanning the decades that separated them. One evening, as she closed the journal, she noticed a small, faded photograph tucked between its pages. It was a portrait of Arnaud and Isabelle, their eyes locked in a gaze that transcended time and space.

Compelled by an irresistible urge, Evelina began to paint a portrait of Isabelle based on the description in Arnaud's journal. As she worked, she felt a strange sense of familiarity, as if she were not just creating an image but reconnecting with a soul long lost. The painting, when completed, hung in her studio like a window to another world.

One misty morning, as Evelina stood gazing at her masterpiece, she heard the sound of footsteps behind her. Turning, she found herself face to face with a man who seemed to have stepped out of Arnaud's journal – tall, with eyes that held the depth of a thousand sunsets and a smile that promised untold stories.

"My name is Luc Duval," he said softly, his voice carrying the cadence of old-world charm. "Arnaud was my grandfather."

Evelina's heart skipped a beat. Luc explained that he had inherited the bookstore and his grandfather's journal. Drawn by an inexplicable force, he had come to Paris to uncover the truth behind Arnaud's unfinished love story.

As days turned into nights, Luc and Evelina shared their love for Arnaud's words, exploring the city's romantic landmarks – the Notre-Dame Cathedral, the Luxembourg Gardens, and the Seine's banks – each place echoing with the echoes of Arnaud and Isabelle's love. They discovered that their own feelings for each other were as timeless and profound as the love described in the journal.

One moonlit night, beneath the Eiffel Tower, Luc took Evelina's hands in his and recited a poem his grandfather had written for Isabelle, altering the words to fit their own story. Tears shimmered in Evelina's eyes as she realized that she had found not just the love of a lifetime but a connection that spanned generations.

In that moment, amidst the twinkling lights of Paris, Evelina and Luc became part of a love saga that transcended time, proving that true love, like the city of lights, never fades. Their story, a modern-day "Love Across Time," became a testament to the enduring power of romance, written not just in words but in the brushstrokes of fate and the whispers of forgotten memories.

Story 12：Destined by Three Lives: A Tale of Eternal Bond

In the quaint village of Loire Valley, nestled amidst the rolling vineyards and ancient castles of France, lived a young woman named Claire de Rocher. Claire, with her cascade of raven-black hair and eyes that mirrored the depth of a moonlit Loire River, was known for her gentle demeanor and insatiable curiosity about the world beyond her village.

Claire's grandmother, Marie, often recounted tales of ancient legends and mystical beliefs, weaving stories of fate and destiny into the fabric of Claire's childhood. One such tale spoke of "Yuan Ding San Sheng" – a Chinese phrase meaning "Destined by Three Lives," which described souls bound together by an unbreakable bond across lifetimes. Marie believed that Claire's destiny was intertwined with someone far beyond the village's borders.
Years passed, and Claire grew into a woman of refined beauty and wisdom. She became a teacher, imparting knowledge to the children of Loire Valley, while her heart yearned for an adventure beyond the familiar vines and cobblestone streets. Unbeknownst to her, fate was already weaving its intricate threads.

In the bustling city of Paris, a young artist named Gabriel Le Noir was struggling to find his true calling. Gabriel, with his tousled chestnut hair and eyes that sparkled with creative fire, was renowned for his captivating paintings that seemed to capture the essence of human emotions. However, despite his success, Gabriel felt an emptiness within, a void that only a deeper connection could fill.
One fateful day, as Claire attended a regional education conference in Paris, she wandered into an art gallery showcasing Gabriel's works. Her breath caught in her throat as she stood before a painting titled "The Echo of Souls." The canvas depicted two figures standing on a hillside, their eyes meeting across a vast, undefined distance, as if yearning for a reunion that transcended time and space. Claire felt an inexplicable connection to the painting, as if she were staring into the eyes of her own soul's reflection.

Intrigued, Claire sought out Gabriel, who was standing nearby, observing his creation with a mixture of pride and longing. Their eyes met, and for a moment, the world seemed to stand still. Claire felt a surge of warmth and familiarity, as if she had known Gabriel for eons.

Over the following weeks, Claire and Gabriel's paths continued to cross, each encounter deepening their connection. They discovered a shared passion for art, literature, and the mysteries of life. Gabriel showed Claire his studio, filled with sketches and paintings that seemed to capture the essence of their burgeoning love before it had even fully blossomed.
One evening, as they sat by the Seine, watching the sunset paint the sky in hues of gold and crimson, Gabriel revealed the inspiration behind "The Echo of Souls." He spoke of an ancient legend his grandmother had told him, one that echoed Marie's tales of "Yuan Ding San Sheng." Gabriel believed that their souls were bound by an unbreakable bond, destined to find each other across the span of three lifetimes.

Claire's eyes widened as she listened, her heart pounding with realization. She shared Marie's stories with Gabriel, their words merging like two rivers converging into one. They realized that their love was not just a chance encounter but a fulfillment of an ancient promise.
As they gazed into each other's eyes, Claire and Gabriel made a solemn vow. They promised to cherish and uphold their bond, to honor the destiny that had brought them together across the vast expanse of time. Their love, like the Loire Valley's vineyards, would grow richer and deeper with each passing season, a testament to the enduring power of fate and the beauty of souls united by an eternal bond.

And so, in the heart of France, amidst the vineyards, castles, and bustling city streets, Claire de Rocher and Gabriel Le Noir's love story unfolded, a timeless tale of "Destined by Three Lives," written in the stars and etched into the hearts of those who believed in the magic of fate.

Story 13: Love Song of 1990: A Timeless Melody

In the quaint, cobblestone streets of Berlin, Germany, during the twilight of the 1980s, lived a young woman named Elara Bergmann. Elara, with her cascade of wavy chestnut hair and eyes that mirrored the depth of a stormy sea, was known for her captivating voice and insatiable passion for music. She sang in the local choir, her melodies echoing through the city's historic landmarks, filling the air with an ethereal beauty.

Elara's heart, however, yearned for something more. She dreamed of performing on grand stages, her voice resonating with audiences worldwide. But Berlin, still healing from the scars of division, offered limited opportunities for an aspiring singer.

Meanwhile, in the bustling city of Hamburg, lived a young musician named Max Schmidt. Max, with his tousled black hair and eyes that sparkled with creative fire, was a talented pianist and composer. His compositions were a blend of classical elegance and modern innovation, capturing the essence of the changing times. Max, too, harbored dreams of fame and recognition, but like Elara, faced obstacles in realizing his aspirations.

Their paths were destined to converge. In 1990, as the Berlin Wall crumbled, symbolizing the reunification of Germany, a sense of renewal and possibility swept through the nation. It was in this transformative year that Elara and Max's lives intertwined.

Elara had been invited to perform at a charity concert in Hamburg, organized to celebrate the new dawn of unity. Max, too, was among the performers, showcasing his latest compositions. As Elara sang, her voice soaring through the concert hall, Max was captivated. He felt an inexplicable connection to her melodies, as if her songs were echoing his own unspoken dreams.

After the concert, they met. Max introduced himself, his eyes reflecting a mix of admiration and curiosity. They spoke of music, dreams, and the changes sweeping through their country. Hours passed, and as dawn broke over the Hamburg harbor, they realized that they had found a kindred spirit in each other.

Their friendship blossomed into a deep, abiding love. They wrote songs together, their melodies reflecting the joy, sorrow, and hope of their shared journey. Max's piano compositions complemented Elara's soulful vocals, creating a harmony that seemed to transcend time and space.
As their love grew, so did their careers. They performed together, their concerts drawing sold-out crowds. Their music, a blend of classical and modern, resonated with audiences worldwide, becoming a symbol of unity and renewal.

But life, as it often does, threw challenges at them. As their fame grew, so did the pressures of their demanding schedules. Misunderstandings and separations tested their bond, but their love remained steadfast. They learned to cherish each moment they shared, to find joy in the simple things, and to trust in the strength of their connection.

Years passed, and as they looked back on their journey, they realized that their love had become a timeless melody, echoing through the decades like a timeless song. They named their greatest hit "Love Song of 1990," a tribute to the year that brought them together and the love that had endured through the years.

And so, in the heart of Germany, amidst the changing tides of history and the enduring beauty of music, Elara Bergmann and Max Schmidt's love story unfolded, a timeless melody that resonated with the world, a testament to the power of love and the beauty of dreams fulfilled.

Story 14: Riverside of Longing: A Tale of European Romance

In the picturesque village of Vienne, nestled along the banks of the serene Rhône River in France, lived a young woman named Claire Boulanger. Claire, with her cascade of wavy chestnut hair and eyes that mirrored the depth of the river's waters, was known for her gentle demeanor and insatiable passion for music. She played the piano with a finesse that seemed to draw the very soul of the river into her melodies, filling the air with an ethereal beauty.

Claire's heart, however, harbored a secret longing. She dreamed of finding a love that would mirror the timeless beauty of the Rhône, a love that would transcend the mundane and touch the very essence of her soul. But Vienne, though enchanting, offered limited opportunities for a young woman seeking such a profound connection.

Meanwhile, in the bustling city of Lyon, lived a young artist named Lucas De Villepin. Lucas, with his tousled black hair and eyes that sparkled with creative fire, was renowned for his paintings that captured the essence of life and love. His works were a blend of realism and impressionism, drawing viewers into a world where emotions and colors intertwined. Lucas, too, harbored dreams of finding a love that would inspire his art, a love that would be his muse and his soulmate.

Their paths were destined to converge. One summer, Claire, seeking inspiration for her music, embarked on a journey along the Rhône River, hoping to capture its essence in her melodies. Lucas, on the other hand, had been commissioned to paint a series of landscapes depicting the river's beauty. As fate would have it, they both chose the same serene stretch of the river, near Vienne, as the setting for their respective creations.

It was there, amidst the whispering waters and the golden hues of sunset, that they met. Claire was seated at her piano, her fingers dancing over the keys as if guided by an unseen force. Lucas, standing nearby, was captivated by the beauty of her melodies and the serene grace of her presence. He approached her, his heart pounding with a mix of admiration and anticipation.

They spoke of their passions, their dreams, and the beauty of the river that had brought them together. Hours passed, and as the stars began to twinkle in the night sky, they realized that they had found a kindred spirit in each other. Their connection was immediate and profound, as if they had known each other for lifetimes.

Their love grew, nurtured by the gentle waters of the Rhône and the endless beauty of the French countryside. They created together, Claire's melodies inspiring Lucas's paintings, and Lucas's visions inspiring Claire's compositions. Their love was a symphony of colors and notes, a harmonious blend of two souls finding each other amidst the chaos of the world.

But life, as it often does, threw challenges at them. As their careers flourished, so did the demands of their schedules. Separations and misunderstandings tested their bond, but their love remained steadfast. They learned to cherish each moment they shared, to find joy in the simple things, and to trust in the strength of their connection.

Years passed, and as they looked back on their journey, they realized that their love had become a timeless melody, echoing through the decades like a song of longing and fulfillment. They named their favorite spot along the Rhône "Riverside of Longing," a tribute to the place that had brought them together and the love that had endured through the years.

And so, amidst the whispering waters of the Rhône and the endless beauty of the French countryside, Claire Boulanger and Lucas De Villepin's love story unfolded, a timeless tale of European romance, a symphony of love and inspiration that resonated through the ages.

Story 15: The Eternal Bond of Elena and Lucian

In the quaint village of Villeneuve, nestled between rolling hills and dense forests in the heart of France, lived a young woman named Elena D'Arcy. Elena was known for her compassionate nature and radiant beauty, traits that endeared her to everyone in the village. Her emerald-green eyes sparkled with curiosity and warmth, reflecting the love she had for life and the people around her.

Not far from Villeneuve was the elegant château of Lucian De Ville, a man of noble birth and unmatched charm. Lucian, with his chiseled features and cascading raven-black hair, was the embodiment of sophistication and grace. Despite his wealth and status, Lucian was humble and kind, always ready to lend a helping hand to those in need.

One fateful spring day, Elena ventured into the forest to gather herbs for the village's elderly healer, Madame Claire. As she wandered deeper into the woods, she stumbled upon a hidden glade bathed in golden sunlight. There, sitting on a moss-covered rock, was Lucian, playing a haunting melody on his violin. The music enveloped Elena in a warm embrace, stirring emotions she had never felt before.

Transfixed by the beauty of the moment, Elena approached cautiously, not wanting to disturb the enchanting symphony. Lucian noticed her presence and paused, his instrument falling silent. Their eyes met, and in that fleeting instant, time seemed to stand still. A connection, deep and unspoken, was forged between them.

"You must be Elena," Lucian said softly, his voice smooth like velvet. "I've heard much about your kindness and beauty."

Elena blushed, feeling a strange flutter in her chest. "And you must be Lucian. Your music... it's like nothing I've ever heard."

Their conversation flowed naturally, blending like the notes of a symphony. They spoke of dreams, aspirations, and the simple joys of life. Hours passed unnoticed, and as the sun began to set, casting a golden hue over the glade, they knew that something profound had happened between them.

From that day on, Elena and Lucian's paths crossed frequently, whether at village festivals, charitable events, or simply in the hidden glade where they first met. Their bond grew stronger with each passing day, nurtured by shared laughter, whispered confidences, and unspoken glances filled with love.

However, their romance was not without obstacles. Lucian's family, steadfast in their beliefs of arranged marriages and alliances, disapproved of his relationship with Elena, viewing her as too common for their esteemed lineage. Similarly, Elena faced criticism from those who believed she was merely seeking to elevate her social status by associating with Lucian.

Despite the challenges, Elena and Lucian remained steadfast. They found solace in each other's arms, drawing strength from their undying love. In secret, they planned their future, dreaming of a life where love would triumph over prejudice and tradition.

One starlit night, as they sat beneath the ancient oak tree in the glade, Lucian took Elena's hands in his, his eyes burning with determination. "Elena, my love, I cannot bear to be apart from you any longer. Will you marry me, and let us build a life together, regardless of what the world may think?"

Tears of joy streamed down Elena's cheeks as she nodded, her voice breaking with emotion. "Yes, Lucian. My heart belongs to you, and I will face any challenge to be with you forever."

Their wedding was a simple yet beautiful ceremony, attended only by their closest friends and family who believed in their love. As they exchanged vows under the open sky, the stars seemed to shimmer brighter, celebrating their union.

Years passed, and Elena and Lucian's love grew stronger with each passing day. They became the beacon of hope and inspiration for many, proving that true love can conquer all. Their story, etched in the annals of Villeneuve, became a legend—a testament to the enduring power of love, unyielding and eternal, just like their bond.

And so, Elena and Lucian lived happily ever after, their hearts intertwined in an eternal bond of love, forever cherishing the moment they first met in the hidden glade of Villeneuve.

Story 16: Charming Moments that Enchanted the City: The Tale of Elena and Lucian

In the charming city of Paris, renowned for its romantic ambiance and timeless beauty, lived a young woman named Elena Villeneuve. Elena was a painter, capturing the essence of life through her vibrant canvases. Her works were celebrated for their depth of emotion and intricate detail, drawing inspiration from the enchanting moments she witnessed in the city.

Lucian De Clermont, a renowned violinist, had recently returned to Paris after a successful tour across Europe. His music was as enchanting as it was soulful, drawing listeners into a world of passion and longing. He had heard tales of Elena's paintings and the unique way she captured the essence of the city. Intrigued, he decided to visit her gallery.

Upon entering the gallery, Lucian was immediately drawn to Elena's work. The paintings seemed to come alive, whispering stories of love, loss, and hope. As he wandered through the gallery, he felt an inexplicable connection to the art, as if he were seeing fragments of his own soul reflected in the brushstrokes.

It was not long before Elena entered the gallery, her presence as captivating as her art. Lucian's heart skipped a beat as he saw her, her eyes sparkling with the same passion that fueled her paintings. They exchanged a knowing glance, as if acknowledging a connection that transcended the physical world.

That evening, they met for dinner at a quaint bistro near the Seine. As they sipped on wine and enjoyed a meal filled with laughter and conversation, they discovered a shared love for the city and its ability to inspire creativity. They spoke of their dreams, fears, and the pursuit of happiness, finding comfort and solace in each other's words.

From that evening on, Elena and Lucian's bond grew stronger. They met frequently, exploring the city's hidden corners and sharing intimate moments under the city's enchanting skyline. Their love was intense, passionate, and filled with an unspoken understanding that they were meant to be together.

As their relationship blossomed, they began to collaborate on a special project. Elena would paint scenes inspired by Lucian's music, while Lucian would compose pieces inspired by Elena's paintings. Their work became a celebration of their love and the city that brought them together.

One evening, as the sun dipped below the horizon, casting a golden glow over the Seine, Lucian took Elena to a rooftop terrace overlooking the city. The skyline was adorned with twinkling lights, as if the city itself were celebrating their love. Lucian took Elena's hands in his, his eyes filled with sincerity and affection.

"Elena, my love, you have brought color to my life, just as your paintings bring life to the canvas. I want to spend every moment with you, exploring the city's beauty and sharing our dreams. Will you marry me, and let us create more charming moments that enchant the city?"

Elena's eyes filled with tears of joy as she nodded, her voice breaking with emotion. "Yes, Lucian. My heart belongs to you, and I want to spend every moment with you, creating memories that will last forever."

Their wedding was a celebration of love and creativity, attended by friends and family who admired their bond. The ceremony was held in a beautiful art gallery, with Elena's paintings and Lucian's music serving as the backdrop for their special day.

As they danced under the twinkling lights, Elena and Lucian felt an overwhelming sense of gratitude. They knew that their love was special, a bond that was meant to be. They vowed to cherish every moment, to find inspiration in the city's beauty, and to create more charming moments that would enchant the city and their hearts forever.

And so, Elena and Lucian lived happily ever after, their love becoming a legend in the city of Paris. Their story was celebrated as a testament to the enchanting power of love, inspiring countless others to believe in the magic of "Charming Moments that Enchanted the City."

Story 17: Enchanted Ecstasy

In the charming city of Paris, where the Seine whispered secrets to the bridges and the Eiffel Tower stood as a sentinel of romance, lived a young woman named Claire Boulanger. With her cascade of chestnut hair and eyes that mirrored the depth of a midnight sky, Claire embodied the very essence of enchantment. She worked as a florist in a quaint boutique nestled in the heart of Montmartre, surrounded by the fragrance of roses, lilacs, and the subtle hint of freshly baked croissants.

One fateful evening, as the city bathed in the golden glow of street lamps, Claire attended a private gallery opening in the Left Bank. The exhibit featured the works of an elusive artist named Gilles de Versailles, whose paintings captured the essence of Paris—its elegance, its mystery, and its unspoken promises. Gilles was renowned for his ability to render emotions onto canvas, making viewers feel as though they were part of the painting itself.

As Claire wandered through the gallery, her gaze was drawn to a particular piece—a portrait of a woman with eyes closed, lost in a reverie of pure ecstasy. The painting seemed to pulse with life, drawing her closer. She stood before it, mesmerized, feeling as though she were being gently pulled into its depths.

Suddenly, Gilles appeared beside her, his eyes twinkling with mischief and a hint of something deeper. "You seem fascinated by my work," he said, his voice as smooth as velvet.

Claire turned to face him, her heart skipping a beat. Gilles was as enchanting as his paintings, with his dark, wavy hair and eyes that seemed to hold galaxies within them. "Your work is... incredible. It's as though I can feel the emotions of the subjects," she replied, her voice barely above a whisper.

Gilles smiled, his eyes locking onto hers. "That's the magic of art, my dear. It has the power to transport us to realms beyond our imagination."

From that moment on, Claire and Gilles's worlds began to intertwine. Gilles invited Claire to his studio, a haven of creativity and inspiration perched atop a hill overlooking the Seine. There, they shared stories, dreams, and an unspoken understanding that transcended words. Gilles painted Claire, capturing her essence in strokes of color that seemed to breathe life into the canvas. In return, Claire crafted bouquets inspired by Gilles's paintings, each one a testament to their growing bond.

One night, as Paris slept under a blanket of stars, Gilles took Claire to a secret garden hidden behind the Louvre. The garden was a sanctuary of enchantment, with paths winding through beds of blooming flowers and the scent of jasmine filling the air. Gilles led Claire to a small clearing, where a table was set with a candlelit dinner, the food a symphony of flavors.

As they ate, Gilles reached into his pocket and pulled out a small, intricately carved wooden box. He opened it to reveal a necklace, its pendant a delicate heart engraved with the initials "C & G." "Claire, from the moment I saw you, you captivated me. You are my muse, my inspiration. Will you let me share my life with you, in a dance of enchanted ecstasy?"

Claire's eyes filled with tears of joy. She nodded, her heart swelling with emotion. Gilles gently placed the necklace around her neck, his fingers brushing against her skin, sending shivers of delight down her spine.

In that garden, under the watchful gaze of the stars, Gilles and Claire's love took flight, a journey through realms of pure ecstasy. Their bond grew stronger, each moment a testament to the magic of love that could transcend time and space. Paris, the City of Light, became their playground, a canvas where they painted their love story in strokes of passion, tenderness, and an unspoken promise of forever.

Years passed, but Gilles and Claire's love remained as enchanting as the first night they met. They created a sanctuary of love in the heart of Paris, a place where every moment was a celebration of enchanted ecstasy, a dance that would never end.

Story 18: Soul Mates Across the Alps

In the picturesque village of Grindelwald, nestled at the foot of the Jungfrau mountain range in Switzerland, lived a young woman named Elara Schmid. With her cascade of silken chestnut hair and eyes that mirrored the deep blue of the surrounding lakes, Elara was known for her kindness and an insatiable curiosity about the world. She worked as a guide at the local tourist office, sharing her passion for the Alps with visitors from around the globe.

One crisp autumn morning, as the sun painted the peaks of the Jungfrau in hues of gold and crimson, Elara met a man named Felix von Sachsen. Felix was a renowned photographer, traveling through Europe to capture the beauty of its landscapes. His camera was his eyes, through which he saw the essence of a place, its soul.

Felix had heard of Grindelwald's breathtaking views and decided to spend a few days exploring its trails and peaks. As fate would have it, Elara was assigned to be his guide. From the moment they met, there was an undeniable connection, as though they had known each other in some forgotten lifetime.

As they hiked through the lush meadows and towering pine forests, Felix captured the essence of Grindelwald through his lens, while Elara shared stories of the village, its history, and its people. They spoke of their dreams, fears, and the small, seemingly insignificant moments that made life rich and meaningful. Felix spoke of his love for photography, how it allowed him to see the world in ways others couldn't, and Elara talked about her passion for the Alps, how they made her feel both small and infinite at the same time.

Each day, their bond grew stronger, a tapestry of shared experiences and unspoken understandings. They discovered hidden trails, watched sunsets paint the sky in shades of pink and orange, and enjoyed simple meals in cozy mountain huts, surrounded by the warmth of newfound friendship.

One evening, as they sat by a roaring fire in a mountain chalet, Felix took out his camera and showed Elara a series of photographs he had taken of her—her laughter, her thoughtful gaze, the way her hair caught the light. "You have a way of seeing the world that's incredibly beautiful," he said, his voice soft and sincere. "But it's not just the world you see. It's the way you see it—with wonder and kindness. That's what makes these photos special."

Elara's eyes filled with tears, not of sadness, but of a profound understanding. "Felix, I've never felt this way before. It's as though I've known you forever. Like we're... soul mates."

Felix smiled, his heart swelling with emotion. "I feel it too, Elara. There's something about you that resonates with me, something deep and unspoken. It's like our souls recognize each other, even though our minds haven't had the time to catch up."

From that moment on, Felix and Elara's journey became a dance of discovery, a quest to understand the depths of their connection. They traveled together, exploring the beauty of Europe, from the serene canals of Venice to the rugged cliffs of the Irish coast. Each place they visited became a testament to their love, a chapter in a story that was still being written.

Years passed, but Felix and Elara's bond remained as strong as the first day they met. They built a life together in Grindelwald, creating a sanctuary of love amidst the majestic beauty of the Alps. They became each other's muse, inspiring each other to grow, create, and cherish the simple, profound moments of life.

In the end, it wasn't just the breathtaking views of the Jungfrau or the serene beauty of the Swiss countryside that made their life together special.

It was the unspoken understanding, the deep, abiding love that connected their souls, making them true soul mates across the Alps.

Story 19: Eternal Love Affair

In the enchanting city of Paris, known for its romance and charm, lived a young woman named Claire Boulanger. With her cascading waves of chestnut hair and eyes that sparkled like the Seine on a sunny day, Claire was a painter, capturing the beauty of the world through her brushstrokes. Her studio, nestled in the heart of Montmartre, was her sanctuary, where she poured her heart and soul into her art.

One fateful evening, as the city's streets glowed with the soft light of twinkling fairy lights and the aroma of freshly baked croissants filled the air, Claire met a man named Lucien de Bourgogne. Lucien was a violinist, a member of the prestigious Paris Opera Orchestra. His music was his passion, his soul's voice, and he played with a fervor that could move even the most hardened of hearts.

Claire and Lucien's worlds collided at a small, intimate jazz club in the Marais district. Lucien was performing a haunting melody that seemed to capture the essence of Paris's eternal love affair with the arts. Claire, who had stumbled upon the club by chance, was immediately drawn to the music. She felt an inexplicable connection to the piece, as though it were speaking directly to her soul.

After the performance, Claire approached Lucien, her heart pounding with a mix of excitement and nervousness. "Your music... it's like you're speaking to me," she said, her voice trembling.

Lucien smiled, his eyes softening with warmth. "I'm glad you felt that. Music has a way of connecting people in ways words never can."

From that night on, Claire and Lucien's lives became intertwined. They spent countless hours together, exploring the city's hidden gems, sharing meals at cozy bistros, and discussing their art and dreams. Lucien played for Claire, his violin singing melodies that seemed to paint the air with emotions, while Claire painted portraits of Lucien, capturing the essence of his soul through her brushstrokes.

As time passed, their bond grew stronger, evolving into a love that was both passionate and deeply spiritual. They were each other's muse, inspiring each other to create, to grow, and to cherish the beauty of life.

But life, as it often does, threw them a curveball. Lucien was offered a position with a prestigious orchestra in Vienna, a dream opportunity that he couldn't refuse. Claire, too, was offered a scholarship to study painting at an art academy in Florence. Their hearts ached with the thought of being separated, but they knew that this was a chance for them to grow, to chase their dreams, and to become the best versions of themselves.

They promised each other that no matter where they were, their love would remain strong, a beacon guiding them back to each other. And so, with heavy hearts and hopeful spirits, they parted ways, their love affair taking on a new form—one of distance, but not of heart.

Years passed, and Claire and Lucien's lives took them to the farthest reaches of Europe. But their love, like the Seine, flowed endlessly, never faltering, never fading. They wrote letters, shared their art, and spoke of their dreams and aspirations. And every chance they got, they met, their hearts leaping with joy, their spirits rekindling in the presence of each other.

In the end, it wasn't the city of Paris or the enchanting beauty of Europe that made their love affair eternal. It was the depth of their connection, the unspoken understanding, and the unwavering belief in the power of love that transcended time and space. Claire and Lucien's love affair became a testament to the enduring power of love, a love that was truly eternal.

Story 20: Sweet Surprise Attack

In the bustling city of Berlin, Germany, lived a young woman named Emma Schmidt. Emma was a vibrant, spirited individual, with a heart full of dreams and a smile that could light up even the darkest of days. She worked as a pastry chef at a renowned bakery called "Süße Wunder," known for its delicious treats and charming atmosphere.

One sunny afternoon, Emma was busy preparing an elaborate dessert display for the bakery's upcoming grand opening event. She was meticulously crafting chocolate macarons, layering them with a smooth, silky ganache that was her secret recipe. As she worked, she couldn't help but think about the man who had recently stolen her heart—Lucas Krause, a charming and talented photographer who had recently moved to Berlin from Munich.

Lucas had a knack for capturing the beauty in everyday moments, and his work had been featured in numerous prestigious publications. He had recently been hired to take photos of Süße Wunder for their promotional materials, and it was there that he and Emma first met. From the moment they locked eyes, there was an undeniable spark, a connection that neither could explain but both knew was real.

As the days turned into weeks, Emma and Lucas's friendship blossomed into something deeper. They spent countless hours together, exploring Berlin's vibrant streets, sharing meals at cozy cafes, and discussing their dreams and aspirations. Lucas's photos of Emma in the bakery kitchen, her hands covered in chocolate and flour, became some of his most cherished works.

But as much as they loved spending time together, their schedules were often hectic, and finding moments for just the two of them was a challenge.

So, Emma decided to plan a surprise for Lucas, something that would show him just how much he meant to her.

The grand opening of Süße Wunder was the perfect opportunity. Emma spent days perfecting her most intricate and delicious desserts, each one designed to be a visual and culinary masterpiece. And then, she had an idea—she would create a special dessert just for Lucas, something that would be a "sweet surprise attack" to his senses.

On the night of the grand opening, the bakery was buzzing with excitement. Emma's desserts were a hit, with people lining up to taste her creations. Lucas arrived, his camera in hand, ready to capture the magic of the evening. As he took photos of the stunning desserts, Emma led him to a small, secluded table in the corner of the bakery.

"Close your eyes," she instructed, her voice filled with excitement.

Lucas did as he was told, his curiosity piqued. Emma placed a small, beautifully decorated dessert in front of him, then gently took his hand and led it to the spoon. "Now, open your eyes and taste."

Lucas opened his eyes to find a stunning chocolate mousse cake, decorated with delicate edible flowers and a heart-shaped chocolate piece on top. He took a spoonful, and his senses were immediately overwhelmed by the rich, creamy texture and the perfect balance of flavors. It was like a sweet symphony playing on his taste buds, each note harmonizing in perfect unity.

Emma watched as Lucas's eyes lit up with delight, his face breaking into a wide, heartfelt smile. "This... this is incredible," he said, his voice filled with awe.

Emma smiled, her heart swelling with joy. "It's a sweet surprise attack, just for you. I wanted to show you how much you mean to me, and how much I appreciate everything you do."

Lucas's eyes softened with warmth, and he reached out to take Emma's hand. "Thank you, Emma. This means more to me than you could ever know."

From that moment on, "Sweet Surprise Attack" became a special term of endearment between them, a symbol of their love and the sweet, unexpected moments they cherished together. And as they continued to explore Berlin, share meals, and create memories, they knew that their love story was just beginning, filled with endless possibilities and sweet surprise attacks around every corner.

Milton Keynes UK
Ingram Content Group UK Ltd.
UKHW051833011224
451808UK00011B/118